Ambassadors of the Silenced

In loving memory of Elizabeth Armentani who loved to read & write poetry

Ambassadors of the Silenced

Poems by

Alfred Encarnacion

Love always,
Alfred
Stratford, NJ
11/6/16

Kelsay Books

Cover Art:
Monica N. Peluso

ISBN 978-1-945752-01-8

Kelsay Books
Aldrich Press
www.kelsaybooks.com

In memory of Martha and Stephanie Quigley:
When the moon shines bright we say goodnight . . .

Thank you
Jim Daniels, Eugene Gloria,
Maria Mazziotti Gillan
for your blessings

Acknowledgments

American Arts Quarterly: "Back Street"

Common Ground Review: "Jersey Reds"

Connecticut River Review: "Pause En Route"

Crab Orchard Review: "Pearl of the Orient," "Photo of a Filipino-American Dance Party, Girard Manor, New Year's Eve, 1940" and "Following the *Tikgi* Birds" (earlier version)

Edison Literary Review: "My Sister's First Communion Photograph, an Alternate Copy"

Florida Review: "Stepfather" (under the title "Mother's Second Husband Steals Her Old Wedding Band")

Grasslands Review: "The Diving Bell, Atlantic City, 1963"

Hawai'i Pacific Review: "Ambassador of the Silenced" (under the title "For U Sam Oeur")

Home Planet News: "Bulosan Pauses at a Crossroads, 1930"

Indiana Review: "Bulosan Listens to a Recording of Robert Johnson" and "Threading the Miles"

Journal of American Culture: "Bulosan at the Cannery (Rose Inlet, Alaska, 1933)"

LIPS: "No Map Can Hold the Wind"

North American Review: "Cross-Dressing the Dinosaurs"

The Open Boat: Poems from Asian America: "Preface to a Union Speech, Seattle, Autumn, 1933" (under the title "Seattle, Autumn, 1933")

The Outskirts of Karma: "Landscape with Querulous Couple," "My Cat and I Sit Out on the Balcony After Dinner, Watching the Sunset and Pretending We're Famous Poets," "Saying the Names," "Winter Light"

Paterson Literary Review: "After the Summer," "Birthday Elegy, 1995," "Chinese Lanterns," "Hey, Chink," "*In Absentia,*" "It's a Wonderful Life," "She Devil, 1957"

Red River Review (online journal): "Roman a Clef"

Tobeco: "Visiting Cousin Anna at the Masonic Home for the Aged"

Additionally, some of these poems appeared in the following anthologies: *Blues Poems, Identity Lessons, Letters to America, The Open Boat* and *Unsettling America*.

Contents

Three: The *Tikgi* Birds

Four: Winter Light

In Absentia

 I wish my grandfather
on Cebu had given my father a photo

of himself to pass on
to me, his *mestizo* grandson, in America.

        It's lonely inventing a face
to connect myself to a history remote

      as that morning in 1896
when Jose Rizal martyred himself for the Philippines.

Hoy, Rizal! national hero, good secular saint,
             I invoke your name for the umpteenth time:

      I need your spirit, your commitment,
to affirm this unheroic life I live in the present.

Maybe then I wouldn't stare so long in mirrors,
        checking to see if I'm really there.

Sometimes I am.

"Those who speak know nothing;
Those who know are silent"
—Po Ch

"What happens, happens in silence"
—Lisel Mueller

One: Pearl of the Orient

"First there were the men, Filipino men. And though they came from different Philippine islands, when they got here, they called themselves *Pinoys*"

—Peter Bacho

Pearl of the Orient

sounds exotic like a prize
daylily whose leaves
are cool tongues of flame,

whose flowers are yellow
clustering suns. But, no,
it's the name of a seedy bar

in the heart of "Flip Town,"
San Francisco, 1938.
My father is young,

a few years off the boat:
hard, lean, a flake of powdered
sugar on his lip, he straddles

a stool among the drunken
Pinoys who dub him "Freddie
Donuts." Watch him twist,

as if a cruller, the arm of that fat
Illocano who lurks in the red booth,
who wields a thick black stogie,

who shanghais the unwary *flips*
to canneries up north. "Ball-less
bastard," my father shouts

in dialect I cannot understand
as he understands indentured labor,
Alaskan summer, king salmon runs.

2.
Freddie's learned to duck his head, roll with punches,
sidestep manholes that pit these streets of gold.
He bobs & weaves his way through shadows, hungry
for the big time. Knifed by sailors, conned by hookers,
cleaned out by slick J-Town gamblers—he walks the New World
with both eyes open. "You no see too much, you no get too far,"
he warns the young *kaibigans* before he leaves the Pearl.
What he doesn't say is that he's sick of pickup bars,
the razor fights over painted girls with skins as white
as heroin; sick of "Chinese whiskey"—cheap Schenley—
shuffleboard, five card draw, swirling Pall Mall haze.
3.
The moon floats like an island
out on the bay. My father leans

from a pier—his black hair stirred
by wind that sways the Golden Gate—

sees Cebu swept clean by waves
7,000 miles away, smells *carabaos*

of childhood, tastes squid steamed
in banana leaves. Amid morning's maze

of tracks, he'll board a silver train,
start his long trek east with plans

to rake in the big green bucks,
as though some god had spoken:

Pinoy, you must change your life

Photo of a Filipino /American Dance Party, Girard Manor, New Year's Eve, 1940

The photographer uses the widest angle
to capture the shot. Maybe two hundred
guests fill the ballroom decorated tonight
with streamers and bright paraphernalia.
Gala celebration to ring in the New Year

while Europe's on the verge of *blitzkrieg*
and murmurs of thunder spread from off
the Sea of Japan. But the crowd is smiling
with horns and pointed party hats, unperturbed
by the conflict that's unfolding. The women

are white, dressed in long formal gowns
that flare slightly from their waists.
They stand in cliques embracing their dark
escorts—so dapper tonight in slick double-
breasted suits, starched white collars

sprouting black satin bows or perfectly
knotted custom-made silk ties with diamond
tie clips. What makes this blown-up photo
so revealing is not the attraction of opposites
—light and dark, east and west—

but the blind happiness of revelers
poised on the edge of a precipice.
Yet even these festive sleepwalkers,
must soon awaken to the abyss:
world plunged into war. My eyes are pulled

off center by a couple standing in the
far left corner of the crowd—they will
become my parents. How stalwart and calm
my yet-to-be father stares, how radiant
my unpregnant mother, her hand hooked on

his arm, near the stroke of midnight, music
welling up in the musicians' instruments,
the sextet encircling a Christmas tree
on the small bandstand, everyone waiting
for the countdown, the volley of kisses,

the song that begins the Year of the War.

Jersey Reds

This river shines with faces
of my dead like the
countenance of clouds

reflected on water.
My mother young again—
as in the photo, ca. 1953—

at the Whitman Factory,
across the bridge, testing
the quality of sweet dark

chocolates streaming by her
in endless waves, the conveyor
belt relentless as current;

my father decked out
in a snazzy bosun's uniform
the day we tour the docks,

his hands, large and firm,
lift me without effort
to grasp the freighter's

tremendous wheel in a child's
grip, my first flinch
of intimidation. Oh,

what history flows between
then and now! Decade after
decade the Delaware snaked

through the lives of my grand-
father, my aunts and uncle
who slaved for Campbell Soup

in those dim sweat shops
along the Camden riverfront,
far from the lights of Philly.

In peak season, they brought
home bags of Jersey Reds
for my grandmother to slice

and fry with pale milk gravy
in her blackened pans. Tomatoes,
huge and shimmering,

surely rolled through her
dreams like suns rising
and setting in the river.

Mornings, crossing the bridge
on the way to work
I stare down at the water,

dazzled by its cast-off
skin of reflections,
its long crawl out to the sea.

Armistice

The war is over,
they negotiate a peace.

Hurray!

He comes one evening
to collect his things:
the bulging duffel bag,
the ukulele missing
strings, the bosun's
uniform with buttons
bright as stars.

I watch him leave.

He's parked outside
in the teeming rain,
          beneath a tree
twice tattooed by lightning.
Backing from our drive-
way, my father waves
& waves & waves . . .

his face behind the wind-
shield shrinking
to a photo
stuffed inside
a bottle
          lost at sea.

Stepfather

My mother thinks she loves this man
who loathes himself, who drinks too much,
whose first name rhymes with grieve.
Mock orange bushes shake their blooms

with premises of storm. One night, half-lit,
Steve lifts me up to sip beer on his lap:
he holds my rigid body like some ventriloquist
until I wiggle free, wedge between his legs

and plant my teeth with all a dummy's rage.
His body writhes; screams bounce off the walls . . .
My sister claps her hands. My mother stares in silence,
feels a slender band of light encircling her finger.

Somewhere at sea, in noonday sun, aboard
a blistered freighter, my father climbs on deck,
lights a Lucky Strike—inhales, exhales
a perfect ring of smoke.

Roman a Clef

. . . 2 a.m. The woman behind the counter in the White Castle
lights a cigarette, plucks a dollar from the tip cup, catches
her lone customer staring at a bruise purpling her cheek.
Across the street her husband's lit like the jukebox
in the corner of the Blue Moon Bar & Grill. He slouches
on a stool, picks his nose clean, thinks of his stepson's
smooth olive flesh, the scant wiry hairs, the thin dangle
of the pud. Outside snow falls, a frenzy of flakes
the sky can no longer restrain. The waitress dumping grinds
cannot guess why her son has changed, why he practices
silence, studies maps in his room, plotting endless escapes.
She cannot see the knife he grips in bed, how he resists
the undertow of sleep, staring at the nite lite's blue halo
till all is a blur . . . or how sometimes he wakes pinned beneath
someone's heavy breathing, sheets blinding as snowdrifts
in the moonlight. This morning the boy traces a crack—
faint scar—across the face in the mirror, closes his eyes,
imagines the moment a snowflake dissolves like communion
                                        on his tongue.

"Hey, Chink!"

I'm not Chinese, but I hear that salutation
          over & over
          growing up in Fishtown with its surly children,
its stench of slaughterhouses,
its bars with names like Bub's Swank Club,
                  drunks blowing smoke-
     rings in a daze.
Through a thousand grimy windows, I stare
          astonished at the rusting girders
               holding up the El; pigeon
     shit—white as coke
            in a junkie's nose—splotches
sidewalks trashed with newsprint, shards
      of glittering glass, beer cans boys squash
      to make "horse shoes" in the summer sun.
                Chink.
I blame my father for the slanted eyes
          I hide behind sunglasses,
     for hair the color of Chinese ink.
     Mythic father who sailed off in the '50s
taking the fruit of his language: *Visayan,*
      dialect that should fill my mouth with the sweet-
      ness of mango, stings my tongue with its tang
          of strange syllabics.
          Weekends, I'm sent packing
     to Mother's family across the river
               in plush New Jersey townships
where kids clean-cut as Mouseketeers still stare
      or yell: "Hey, Chink!"
But I learn to swallow hard,
          erase my face to blank.

She Devil, 1957

When I was nine the only thing
　　I wanted to be was Joe Boyle,
the blue-eyed, blond-haired angel of St.
　　Anne's Roman Catholic School.
Years I dreamed my days away,
　　longing to know the secret behind
the gift of occidental beauty.
　　My face—not Irish, not welcome—
belonged to a postwar baby
　　with slanted eyes, chubby cheeks,
and waves of squid-black hair.
　　Why wasn't I a golden child
whose life the saints had blessed?
　　Ò, make my eyes round as Joe's
I petitioned the blind god of mirrors;
　　I tried so hard to be that kid,
wanting even the early case of acne
　　that flared-up on his face.
I dabbed my skin with Clearasil *hoping*
　　to raise a crop of tiny zits.
Pimples would make me American!
　　But to no avail: I stayed
a smooth-skinned asian oddball.
　　Sitting alone at a Saturday
show, watching *She Devil,*
　　another budget horror film,
unfold, I imagined changing the way
　　I looked at will like that woman
on the screen who's drunk experimental
　　serum that alters her appearance
from drab brunette to electrifying blonde.
　　But of course her behavior's altered

too, and she grows more ruthless, more evil
        till subdued by pellets of poison gas.
It would take years to learn no secret
        serum could change me to Joe Boyle.
I'd remain that dark and sullen boy
        scribbling pain on scraps of paper,
praying for some private transformation.

Cross-Dressing the Dinosaurs

I couldn't stomach that word *extinction,*
its 3 syllables of finality stuck in my throat.
Saturdays the 5&10s were packed with kids
hunting for their favorite plastic dinosaurs.
How pampered they looked on their prehistoric
shelves—stegosaurus with his tail of spikes,
the jolly duckbilled trachodon, plesiosaurus
had a painted sea to swim in, while pterodactyls
hung from wires above miniature volcanoes
ready to erupt. My friends all grabbed
for tyrannosaur, that Jurassic superstar, but
T-Rex reminded me of "Do Do" Petrosky,
the Webb St. bully who always spit
thick green hockers in your hair.
My pick: brontosaurus, gentle giant,
wader of primordial marshlands, chubby
and good-natured as my friend "Fat"
Heaster, the school screw-up, whom
everyone dumped on, even our nuns.

Bronto, like Fat, was going to be a buddy.
I raced home from school to play our game
"dress-up." No tag, no hide-and-seek, no
stick ball could excite me like dressing up
a dinosaur in my sister's doll clothes.
How fabulous he looked in two pairs of red
high heels! A black velour cape made a chic
statement with a pearl Barbie anklet.
And didn't that long slender neck just cry
out for a necklace improvised from a teeny
diamond tiara? My sister's injunction—
"Make that bastard give back Barbie's

accessories!"—brought a visit from Uncle A.
who sat perplexed in our kitchen
as my mother and aunt explained
the problem. He knew what to say when
we had our chat about not peeping through
the keyhole when my teenage cousin,
with the big boobs, was showering,
or why guys never, never sit down to do
number one like the ladies ("Don't you
damn women teach the boy anything?"
he grumbled, popping a can of Schmidt's.)
But this was different. Dinosaurs in drag?
He laughed like hell and said to me, "Kiddo,
you're odd as a cod." But I was 7 and had
read how climates changed, glaciers spread,
dinosaurs died out. *Extinct.* Did my imagination
need to protest that Ex-word of monumental
proportions? Did I want to dress up
my fears in flamboyant garb and trod
down a glittering runway? Who knows?
Maybe I loved the idea of a long lost behemoth—
with brain the size of a cat-eye marble,
the kind I used to play Fat Heaster for—
putting on a show. Wardrobe! Makeup! Lights!
When you got it, baby, flaunt it!

Out There

He screamed.
    Sometimes in the middle
        of the night. Sometimes
in broad daylight. SCREAM!
    It came without warning,
        without context.

One minute
    the ordinary sounds
        in my aunt and uncle's house—
their voices calm and moderate,
    the clock's complacent ticking in the kitchen,
        a muffled telephone somewhere ringing—
                then
Bob's scream, piercing the wall,
    startling our lives.
        "He's harmless, just a bit... *out there*,"
my aunt would hesitate.
    She felt sorry for Bob,
        their neighbor's odd son,
who couldn't work,
    who once slashed his wrist,
        who always harangued
some invisible companion as he tramped along
    the township streets.

    This was the '60s when
the world seemed lighter
    to bear or being a child
        I was less aware of its
dark weight over the lives
    of those burdened

by pain, rage—their
shrieks falling on clasped ears.
    Neighbors pointed bluntly at Bob
        or made snide remarks when he passed.
"Weirdo," "Retard," "Fruitcake,"
    they dubbed him, and I,
        along with those other stupid children
who mocked him, tossed crab apples
    at his head, though he never
        ceased to smile at us.

        Why didn't I know better?
Those same neighbors stared hard
    at me—my dark hair,
        my Asian features—
their kids socked me for not being "American"
    enough. I should have been
        Bob's staunchest defender,
            not another tormentor.

Decades too late, Bob
    Granger, let me apologize.
        There are moments
now when I feel so alone
    I'm desperate to unleash
        one long anguished scream
through the walls of my own
    life, to announce my distress,
        to announce that I'm there—
yes really, I am out there.

It's a Wonderful Life

The mirror doesn't exactly crack
when I stare intensely into it,
rather my reflection seems pried apart
like one of Picasso's paintings

until I guiltily reassemble it
into the face I've dreamed:
the nose pugged, the cheekbones
lowered, eyelids round as apples

with maybe a faint cleft in the chin.
I guess I still want to be Joe Boyle,
still want to look "American"
—whatever that means or doesn't—

after all these years. Once back
in high school I confessed my secret
to a black friend, Darnell, who shot me
a look and said point-blank,

"You mean you want to be *white*."
And I suppose he was right although
I didn't admit it as I've failed to admit
many things in this life that I've made

bereft of wonder and desperate for grace.

Searching for Signs

I'm becoming accustomed
to my own mortality: the elevated
blood sugar that denotes diabetes,
the strange numbness of foot
that bodes something
ominous on its way.

My hair has thinned like hopes
for a future won by high aspirations,
though I keep trying to climb
a secret Mount Everest.
Each day new wrinkles rewrite
my face, a palimpsest of flesh.

In the world of violent headlines
I negotiate a truce with death,
find solace in my memory,
joy in unlikely places. I flip for love,
heads or tails, with coins
off the eyes of the dead.

Older now than I ever imagined
I search for signs to revise
my life. But the sky breathes smog,
the sea has receded, the earth's grown
toxic and cold. Even the beasts
we worshipped have vanished

into distant constellations.
Cities of glass spiral upward
over the heads of the homeless
who wander the streets, day

and night, hungry for charity
beyond the tokens we toss them.

And last night a man, thin
as the crescent moon, rose
from his cardboard bed
as I passed by the corner.
Frantic, he shouted, "Me! Me! Me!"
over and over like the syllables

of a language
I could no longer claim
as my own.

My Sister's First Communion Photograph, an Alternate Copy

As you can see I've altered the shot,
foregrounding her angelic presence:
white dress, white veil, white gloves
drawn together in perfect prayer. She
is now the shy central figure with
the thin, beautiful face. The man
posing beside her is left anonymous—
torso, trousered legs, part of an arm
snaking around her waist—denied
his head and face and hands, as once he
denied us safety in his drunken house.
It is not my first attempt at revising
history—nor my last. Juxtaposed always
with this photo are those secret snapshots
locked in memory's scrapbook, the ones
you can't see of my sister with his hands
around her—hands I couldn't tear away—
dragging her down the hallway to his room,
dragging her to the kitchen table. He wants
her to grow up to be daddy's big girl.
His left hand grips her hair, yanks
the small head back, the right shovels spoonfuls
of cold mashed potatoes, stiff as communion,
into her mouth. She gags, pleads for him to stop.
Eat! Years later, as if obeying that childhood
command, she'll slowly eat herself to death.
But that's still a lifetime away. Here in the
photographer's studio, she remains innocent
of the anguish that will unfold, remains
the angel of our violent household.
                    In future copies,

I will further prune that man's image
until he is a shadow, an obscure crease
in the curtained backdrop, a mere innuendo
of menace that cannot darken the purity
of this moment.

    —for Steffie

Blessing the House, 1958

"The caged bird sings with a fearful trill"
—Maya Angelou

She works nights at the Bridge Cafe
and has to sleep by day. He smokes,
drinks, rules the house with his iron
hand that strikes again and again,

leaving ruins as in the wake of
a hurricane. Everywhere furniture
overturned, battered doors torn
half-off their jambs, wood splinters

out like bone through broken flesh.
There are window panes with holes
the shape of someone's fist, wallpaper
hangs in tattered strips, roaches dash

across the kitchen's scarred linoleum,
its bright pattern long since worn away
to gray. Nothing works. Static plagues
the radio like a perpetual sore throat;

the picture on the small tv shrinks
each passing day until it flares black
as her swollen eye, and the Zenith stares
blindly in a corner of the living room.

I don't know why the caged bird sings,
but I find a tablet and begin to write:
the only way I can douse my rage,
the only way I can bless that house.

Two: Ambassadors of the Silenced

I sat at the bare table in the kitchen and began piecing together the mosaic of our lives in America. Full of loneliness and love, I began to write.

—Carlos Bulosan, *America Is in the Heart*

Threading the Miles

In Memoriam, Carlos Bulosan (1911-1956),
Pinoy poet, novelist, activist

I move to the window
that's filled with wet light.

I thread a small needle and
set to work, noting how rain
falls so easily like sewing a rip

in the breast of this shirt, not
taking it off, though I'm risking

bad luck. I should be writing
a poem about Carlos Bulosan,
his exile in America:

how he faced the rain, the
violence, how he made *adobo*

with scrap meat from garbage,
how he bummed miles to find work,
dreaming of the family he'd left

on Luzon. What stitches our dreams
through our bodies like threads

through cloth? Each dream,
each stitch, a solitary act,
a lonely art. While I sew,

a woman walks by in the rain
outside—old, slow, oblivious

as stone. Vietnamese, maybe
Cambodian. Dressed like the poor
in such jarring garments: orange

and purple colliding with green.
She carries a Pepsi, a wet bag

from Wendy's and no umbrella.
She walks in a daze, yet
with deep resignation. I know

how some of us move by rote,
as if the light of our minds hovered

in other places. I imagine paddies,
jungles, thunderous plateaus
across the sea, ominous journeys

undertaken in private when parts
of our lives wash away or collapse

around us, leaving chasms and
no direction but the long road
into darkness. The tear

in the cloth disappears. I pull
the thread tight, as though

stitching my heart, sew in the knot.
When I look out the window
the old woman has vanished, lost

in the rainy afternoon haze. Somehow
I'm stricken, thinking of miles

so cruel they boggle the mind.
Wait. Come back. Share with us...
And Bulosan tramps down the highway

through yellow fog in the California
rain, on his way to pick fruit

in the Yakima Valley. 1936.
The year of pariah: *Pinoys* gunned down
in the streets of white towns.

Fog starting to lift, clean sun
burning through . . . . This young man—

mid-twenties, beautifully alone,
his wet clothes ragged,
his boots caked with red mud—

slips a flat, amber bottle
out of his pocket, takes

a deep swig, takes another.
The road stretches forward
as from a spool of black thread,

disappears through the eye
of a needle.

Garland for Bulosan

"What was Bulosan like? A tiny person with a limp . . . shy, generous, terribly poor, terribly exiled in California...a Filipino patriot, a touch of the melodramatic about him, given to telling wildly improbable stories about himself, disappearing from Southern California for months at a time, probably to work in a Seattle or Alaska cannery . . . . If I were a good Christian I think I might label him a saint, for he radiated kindness and gentleness"

—John Fante, novelist and screen writer

1.
Bulosan Pauses at a Crossroads, 1931

"It was now the year of the great hatred: the lives of Filipinos
   were cheaper than those of dogs"
                              —*America is in the Heart*

Don't ask me the places I've been but the miles
I've traveled, highways that stretch from the false glitter
of Mardi Gras to the dark canneries of Alaska. Don't ask
me the lives I've left behind but the voices I carry with me,
songs of the shanghaied immigrants who labor,
day after day, knee-deep in fish heads and gutted gore,
their eyes dyed with the blood from dynasties of king
salmon. Yes, I've seen *Pinoys* starving outside chop suey
joints in railroad towns along the coast. No, I won't forget
comrades gunned down in picket lines, their stiff bodies
dumped and burned in secret bonfires on the outskirts
of Exeter and Watsonville. Have you passed towns
too brutal to appear on any roadmap, too obscene
to reference in any speech? I tramp the roads
of your poor, your anonymous—these blue roads
that bleed from your paper heart, America.

2.

Bulosan Rides the Rails

"America is also the nameless foreigner, the homeless refugee,
the hungry boy begging for a job"
                                        —*America is in the Heart.*

Let this boxcar roll through west coast
        thunder;
                let lightning
sizzle down my throat,
                ignite the blues in my belly.

Let hunger wrap her long legs around me
        and moan. Let sheaves of poems gather,
                a feast of words.

Once the Word is made flesh
let me hasten to eat.

  If I find no streets of gold,
                just cold white faces—
    sheriffs, townsmen, vigilantes
                waving clubs: "Move on, *flip,*
  Americans work here"—

let my face, shaped by the wind, be a worn
                map of train routes,

the lines of my brow
miles of rusted track

        a *Pinoy* travels each day,
                his knapsack a hive
                        of lost voices

49

3.
Bulosan Listens to a Recording of Robert Johnson

You sing a hard blues,
black man. You too have been driven:
a tumbleweed in harsh wind.
I close my eyes, your voice rolls
out of the delta, sliding
over flashy chords
that clang like railroad tracks.

Gotta keep movin'
Gotta keep movin'
Blues fallin' down like hail

One summer
I worked the *wash-lye*
section of a cannery up north,
scrubbed schools of headless fish,
breathed ammonia fumes so fierce
I almost floated off
like the arm of a friend,
chopped clean at the elbow
by a cutter's machine.

Gotta keep movin'
Gotta keep movin'
Hellhound on my trail

We are the lost men, *kaibigan,*
our pockets empty of promise.

Mississippi/California—
bad luck conspires against us,
cheap wine stings in our veins.
We reel drunk and bitter
under the white, legal sun.
Robert Johnson/Carlos Bulosan—
our names so different,
our song the same.

4.
Bulosan at the Cannery
(Rose Inlet, Alaska, 1938)
"I promised myself that I would read ten thousand books...
I plunged into books, boring through the earth's core,
leveling all seas and oceans, swimming in the constellations"
—*America is in the Heart*

House of blood and scattered bones... Cascades of fish
from the Bearing Sea flap down on rusted escalators,
ammonia fumes pool in yellow clouds above our heads.
Too beat to cough or choke we reach to scale and clean
by rote... I know this cannery—its stench, its crude
rigid machinery—is an old fisherman's brain, swimming
with shadows, each of us a thought desperate to escape...
Or is this a circle of Dante's hell? At night, in my bunk, I sneak
the Masters: Alighieri, Whitman, Eliot... Summer's the cruelest
season; up here sunset stalls forever, cold raw light flooding
this isle of melting snow, till the moon rises blister-red
in the west. Sometimes in starlight we scrub the stink
of salmon from our bodies, mill around the makeshift field,
start a baseball game or fight. Sometimes we're joined

by tribal girls with Russian names and Indian smiles.
All day they toil beside us; at night they slip beneath
us, lonely as she-wolves. The pups that they will birth?
White bosses call them mongrels, and shamans
will not trust the progeny of two worlds,
fear they'll foretell the village vacant, its totems
tumbled in the wind. We, *Alaskeros,* know their blood
sizzles with our passion, their eyes reflect the cold moon
of their mothers' lives. These children will grow up
to be perfect outcasts. I imagine them marching in rage
from Rose Inlet to Seattle—across the vast, icy terrain—
a band of Asian-Alaskan misfits, prophets born
out of wedlock, out of the tumult of fire and snow.

5.
Preface to a Union Speech,
Seattle, Autumn, 1933

Once more the leaves fall,
flecked with messages
from the dead. Their spiraling
descent signaturing winter:
Alaskeros tremble, terrified
as vagrants of the cold
hissing language of rain,
of wind policing this city.
These days I note
a firm hesitation
before I write, as before
I awake I seem to hold onto

the last thread of sleep
as it's pulled into light
through the blue eye of morning.
Now it's late afternoon.
Soon the moon will rise
from the sea's gnarled mist,
a yellow beacon. I try to hide
my shame in measures of song
as I witness lives squandered
in dance halls and gambling
houses... vats of bootleg
whiskey fermenting...
dens filled with secret opium
dreams... and Chinatown Roses,
with cash-only-smiles, shimmer
at windows, grimy with sin.
But I'm torn by men who wander
streets like tattered ghosts,
women huddled in shadows,
stirring pots of thin soup,
and that child who knelt
one night in a lot,
strangely lit by a bonfire,
who feasted on nothing
but dry, scraggly leaves
and smiled as she hymned
to Our Lady of Flames...
How weather this grief
that numbs into silence?

How may my pen invoke
beauty, not anger?
Nothing inside me feels
tempted to sing. Unless
grievance is song. Fierce
scrape of dead leaf
against leaf, music.

6.
Postcard from the Klamath Falls Jailhouse
> "I came to know afterward that in many ways it was a crime
> to be a Filipino"
>> —*America is in the Heart*

I woke up today at six o'clock,
a clot of sunrise stuck
to the window like blood.
                    Outside,
the morning whistle
                    screamed.
Inside, each cell tore open
like a wound.

7.
Notes from the Los Angeles County Hospital
> "I began to cough violently and could not stop. I rushed to the bathroom
> and bent over the washbowl, coughing out blood...At first I did not realize
> the extent of the disease"
>> —*America is in the Heart*

A decade of changing weather
has changed me for the worse.

Ten years of hopping freights
has brought me to nowhere
but, here, these lonely
hallways, white rooms
with rows of iron beds...
             *

Day after day I lie in a swirl of sheets
in a state of sanitized grace and listen
as men cough up their lives
in TB wards around me...
             *

These mornings of rain—
the hemorrhaged sky,
the hospital porch
empty as my journal—
I think of Basho
        drizzly June—
        long hair, face
        sickly white
and fear I start on
another journey,
my lungs growing
dark with prophesy...
             *

             America,
who's sung your soil,
poet of the Imperial Valley,
its acres of ripening crops;
picked your fruits—

orange, apple, grape—
dreaming in two languages.
Who's wept in the stench
of slaughterhouse & cannery.
Been your salt of the earth,
jack-of-all-trades, ghost
shadow of the harvest...
                 *
Let me spit up words
like blood, fill the pages
of unpublished books.
Let my chapters
be the biography
of the *Pinoy* who flowed
endless as Pacific waves
to these shores. Let me
dream my way back
to a beach on Luzon
where a father teaches
his son how to net
the sweet shrimp,
wrap them in banana
leaves, sizzle them
over coals—so far
from the factory
town I live in now,
its ragged workers,
its dried-out earth,
its rusted machinery
dead in the wind . . . .

8.
Obit: Carlos Bulosan (a found poem)
Deathdate: *11 September 1956, Seattle*
Birthplace: *Philippines*
Address: *Unknown*
Occupation: *Writer*
Hobby: *Famous for jungle salad served*
during Foreign-Born Committee dinners
Estate: *One typewriter, a twenty-year-old suit,*
unfinished manuscripts, worn-out socks
Finances: *Zero*
Beneficiary: *His people*

Ambassador of the Silenced

for U Sam Oeur

"Whoever degrades another degrades me,
    And whatever is done or said returns at last to me."
                         —Whitman

The evening you read
at Borders, the sky
grew so radiant the river
burned with new light.

A small audience sat
entranced by your chants
in *Khmer*, following as best
it could the English

version of your poems.
What nightmares you wailed
sad survivor
of the Pol Pot regime:

your home ransacked,
its library burned;
your family carted off
to concentration camps;

two unborn daughters yanked
like hares from their mother's
womb, buried on a bank
of the Mekong River.

No wonder you had visions
of the *Krasang* tree crying
out against the *Utapats,*
of Buddha's visitation

in the guise of a cobra.
No wonder you recited
lines from *Leaves of Grass*,
praised democracy as a god,

your voice somehow pruned
of rancor. After the reading
we spoke to you briefly,
mumbling our platitudes.

Days later someone
carved *U Sam* into a tree
above Whitman's tomb,
a blossoming tree

of names and initials
rooted in the earth.

The Lonesome Death of Hattie Carroll, an Addendum

"What happened . . . to Zanzinger?"
— Martin Carthy, folksinger

William Zanzinger killed poor Hattie Carroll
with a cane that he twirled round his diamond-
ring finger . . . The old Dylan song still
chills me—a black maid brutally slain,

a man of dazzling wealth and no remorse,
a judge's insipid half-year sentence—
as I listen to Martin Carthy and wonder,
as he, what's become of young William.

Intrigued by that question I search the Net
for days. Secretly I hope for some clean
transformation. Perhaps he's renounced
the privileged life, scattered his wealth

in parishes of the poor, devotes
himself to the championing of those
whom he once so cruelly caned. How
stupid to imagine some men good:

the arrogant eye cannot see the faces
of the scarred, the voice raised in command
cannot whisper for forgiveness,
the hand that feels no shame will crush

the heads of the hapless time and again.
I read a recent online article: *Zanzinger,*
now a landlord, exploits and beats
black tenants on land he doesn't own . . .

O William, Sweet William, whom a generation
of folk fans learned to loathe, I see you
slouched on a LA-Z-BOY in your Maryland
mansion, watching the Orioles win on TV—

you rarely recall a woman named Hattie Carroll;
you've never listened to any damn Dylan songs.

Three: The *Tikgi* Birds

Following the *Tikgi* Birds

1.

Those islands were always there waiting for my imagination to claim them. Despite the fact that I was removed geographically and emotionally from the languages and cultures that thrived throughout that archipelago thousands of miles away, the islands had somehow already claimed me. Sometimes I'm astonished when I think back on the years I tried to ignore them—refusing to recognize them as a homeland, attempting to obliterate any awareness of the Philippines from my consciousness. What had I in common with those dark, squat foreigners who dwelt there? It was a mere accident of birth—an unwanted racial legacy—that linked me to that place. Whatever family I had there had long been lost. As far as I was concerned, those islands could sink back into the sea, like the lost continent of *Mu.*

2.

Though prepared to repress a part of my racial heritage, I could not ultimately escape it. Growing up *mestizo*—half-blood—in a working-class Irish and Polish neighborhood in Philly, I knew from an early age I was both a part of and apart from the people with whom I shared my life. My parents divorced when I was two; I had contact with only my mother's side—the white side—of the family. I lived with her, her husband, their daughter. *Father,* for me, was merely a word, an abstract term I could not emotionally comprehend. I never thought of it in connection with my mother's husband, an abusive, self-destructive alcoholic, and I could never quite connect it to that enigmatic figure that sent child support checks at irregular intervals. Occasionally his name and picture appeared in the newspaper (for years senior man on a team of steeplejacks assigned the perilous custodianship of the clock tower at City Hall) and I would stare with vague curiosity at the newsprint likeness of a stocky, oriental-looking laborer, a man whose job it was to clean the grimy face of an oversized pocket watch, but who couldn't, in thirteen years, spare a day for a visit.

3.

I decided that my parents' marriage had been a terrible mistake—after all they did divorce—so why should I have to bear the burden of their error? The idea that I was the product of a biracial experiment that went wrong—a kind of Frankenstein monster my parents created—obsessed me every waking moment. I was, as one of my childhood companions informed me one day, the only one on our street not "really white," but since my mother and her husband and daughter were "Americans" he supposed it didn't matter that my father was "probably a chink or something." Not only did I feel ugly and foreign, I also was convinced that I carried "bad blood" that must never be passed on to anyone else. When I told my relatives all this, they stared at me with incomprehension, "Why would being Filipino bother you?" they asked. I was silent.

4.

Then I found Bulosan.

I would have liked to have stumbled upon him while wandering around the library on some rainy afternoon in May; I would have liked *America is in the Heart* to have suddenly fallen off the shelf and opened at my feet. But, as it happened, a Filipina girl I met while working in a Center City department store first mentioned Carlos Bulosan to me over lunch one day. Erlinda said that he embodied for her "the *Pinoy* spirit"; she later loaned me his personal history *America is in the Heart.* It was the book I'd been waiting for all my life without knowing it. I found a passionate, meticulous, exhilarating documentation of one man's struggle for self-identity amid the political turmoil of the West Coast during the depression era. It was an eloquent indictment of the systematic racism that threatened the physical, emotional and spiritual lives of the sixty thousand *Pinoys* (immigrant Filipinos) who had migrated to the United States by the mid-thirties.

5.

But more important to me, reading Bulosan's account of his life was like finding some secret journal written by my father long ago and left behind as a gift for me. I was struck by the similarities between the two men: they were approximately the same age (both born in the Philippines, circa 1911-12); they were autodidacts, having been denied a formal education (my father went to second grade, Bulosan to third); they were Third World emigrants who had attempted, each in his own way, to become fully integrated with the new (and often threatening) world they had entered. But whereas my father was supposedly reticent about his past, Bulosan was generously open about his earlier life. I remembered my mother telling me how she once threw out a "terrible book" belonging to my father. She said it was *Mein Kampf,* but I wondered if it had not been *Das Kapital.* Had my father been a young Marxist on the West Coast? Had he ever met Bulosan? That was an incredible thought! But whether their paths ever crossed or not, I felt a closeness to my father, the people and places that had spawned him, I never imagined possible. Through Bulosan we had, in a sense, finally met.

6.

I began to reassess my own past: perhaps being *mestizo*, a product of two different but equally significant cultures, was a blessing in disguise, perhaps it allowed me certain insights I would not have were it not for the circumstances of my birth. Instead of merely resigning myself to my racial background, accepting it as a troubling but irrevocable fact, I suddenly wanted to celebrate it in all its dichotomous nature.

In the "Bulosan Poems," a series of dramatic monologues that had been welling up inside me for a long time, I tried to merge myself emotionally and spiritually with Carlos in order to invent a voice that by the duality of its nature was compelled to take issue with the assumptions of White America. I wanted to imply that he/I was challenging the validity of this country's attitudes and biases, because to a Third World sensibility, such as Bulosan's, Western Civilization itself was simply an extended myth: how binding could any of the values it engendered be?

By juxtaposing the myth of America with an earlier, more indigenous one, a kind of tension might be created, a released energy by which the synthesis of two opposing identities might be accomplished. Thus a new identity could emerge, one that exalts in a balance of contradictions, of exclusion and inclusion, of exile and habitation, of East and West.

7.

In an anthology of world folktales I came across "The *Tikgi* Birds," an entrée from the Philippines. The story goes like this: Old farmer, on the verge of ruin because his family had run away, sat weeping in his rice field one evening at sundown. He knew the rice had ripened but he had no one to cut and bundle it for him. A flock of *Tikgi* birds appeared and circled around him three times. They told him to build a spirit house for the *Sayang* Ceremony and they would harvest his field for him. The farmer hesitated, for he was riddled with doubt, but finally followed the birds' instructions, and the next evening when the *balau*, the spirit house, was built the *tikgis* appeared again. They told him the rice crop was all bundled and stored in the granary and that he would be able to sell it and pay his taxes. The farmer began to weep with joy, but the *tikgis* told him that he must do one more thing to complete their magic. He was to walk behind them as they flew toward a great *bana-asi* tree growing near the forest. When he reached the tree he saw the birds had landed in a circle around it, and he was told not to speak but to close his eyes and clap three times. Without question the farmer obeyed and when he again opened his eyes the *tikgis* had transformed themselves into his lost family. Their souls had been held captive within the bodies of the birds because of some old transgression and had been set free only because of the faith the farmer showed in obeying their instructions. As the moon rose over the island, the man and his family were reunited again.

8.

Driving to Marlton one fall evening to see my sister Lilyan, I easily imagined that the dusky fields along Route 70 were uncut fields of rice. I imagined that the flocks of sparrows I saw wheeling across the New Jersey sky were the fabled *tikgi* birds. I imagined pulling over to the side of the road and walking through the thick white dew, following the *tikgis* to a *bana-asi* tree at the edge of a forest. With a perfect faith I would close my eyes, clap my hands three times and the birds would burst from their feathers, revealing themselves as the family I thought long lost. There, with the full moon rising over the branches of the tree, they would speak to me, neither in English nor *Visayan* but in a new language I could barely describe. Image after image they would fill me like a granary with what was essential, until I was overflowing . . .

Four: Winter Light

in memory of my mother

Winter Light.

1.
The Diving Bell, Atlantic City, 1963

We're locked inside
a crowded metal
shell hunkered
deep in the gray
Atlantic. I hunger
for the exotic, expect
the silver blur
of sharks with ivory
teeth. No dice.
We see no fish,
no plants in
this dark bowl
of saltwater. At last
the bell begins
its rise toward
the floating
light...

30 years later
we surface
in a hushed white
room; nurses like
angelfish stream
past the bed
where you
struggle behind
a respirator
mask. I listen
to your breaths
ebb farther
apart, imagine

a bell—stranger
than the one
we once rode—
drawing the sick
up out of their
deathbeds

to enter

its chamber
of amber sea-
light. Drowned
in fathoms of cold
sunken gloom, I see
a shadow flicker,
a sleek fin circle
the room.

2.
Winter Light

You're gone.

The severance seems almost surgical:
quick, deft, no loose ends. The phone
rings, a nurse's voice breaks the news.

Our insufficient grief . . .

I want something dramatic:
calamities of such proportion
they'll tear the earth apart.

Snow falls quietly.

The first moment we see you dead
an immense absence begins
to insinuate itself. I feel

the cool stiffening flesh

of your body in the hospital
bed and think, *this is fact,*
hard irrevocable fact

On the window sill

yellow chrysanthemums bloom
in the flared green vase,
unperturbed by the occasion.

Outside streets whiten

in the winter light, wind stirs
the bones of naked trees,
footprints, clear and stark,

fill again with snow.

3.
After the Funeral

I drive down the highway
fueled by my disbelief
　　—she's gone—
not caring where I'm headed
so long as there are hills
and mists and wide desolate
spaces. Denver, PA:
the pike courses through it
like a thick artery. Motorists
spend the night at the Holiday
Inn, drive away the next morning
and never look back. But I'm here
to get drunk on deserted Main
Street, in half-vacant stores,
shops with useless antiques;
here to find a lone road up
through the hills that huddle
like gravestones in the shadows
at dusk. I pass the old cemetery
sprawled on a knoll,
a cluster of houses,
a few abandoned cars,
a row of mailboxes
with letters now rust.
The mist rises from ditches.
The sun sinks in the pines.
I park high on a ridge
as snow starts to fall

and drift over the ground
like brilliant blank paper
torn into scraps,
lost in the wind.

4.
The Chinese Lanterns
—a type of plant belonging to the *asteracea,*
    or everlasting, family

"We didn't bond,"
my sister says
when I ask again
if she misses her.

The answer's honed
as the metal spade
my neighbor needs
to turn his soil.

We're sitting
on the edge of lawn
in early spring,
sipping wine.

For three months
I've felt collapse
and shock,
rupture

at the heart
of *being.*

But time continues
like an intricate plot
filled with additions
and deletions, sudden
crises and denouements.
My sister describes

the brittle child
inside herself,
the one who felt
bereft of love.

"I just can't feel
your sense of loss."
But it's presence
we both should feel:

how the dead
insinuate themselves
in the minds of the
living with such

tender bravado,
as in my neighbor's
flowerbed amid
undistinguished

shrubs, the delicate/
extravagant chinese
lanterns, a kind
of everlasting...

5.
Composing for the Dead

Was it only a year ago we quarreled so cruelly?
I ruined your last Xmas as your death's doomed
this one for me. *Your death*—strange
to imagine, stranger to write. Only a year
since our voices clashed in some altercation
I'd have forgotten by now if not for your death.
Once more that incongruous phrase...
The days grow short, the weather cold.
Estranged from sleep, I court the company
of the dead, spend hours composing
songs to those who once were living.
I need to believe what the earth confiscates
is dross, that familiar ritual can return us
to the past. Soon I'll fill the house
with carols, start the spinning wheel
that will shower your aluminum tree
from the '60s with so much color,
so much light.

6.
Birthday Elegy, 1995

Before the gates are shut,
    I must bring you a rose
swaddled in baby's breath.

    For two birthdays
you've lain in a husk
    of impenetrable silence.

But 24 months ago,
   you woke late
on your birthday

   and smiled at us
amid the cards and bright
   packages we'd wrapped.

Today I've come alone
   from your blank rooms,
to be with you.

   What can I relish now
but dreams and photos
   filled with your presence?

What can I bring
   so late in the day
in this last decade

   of a dwindling century
but one rose, singular
   and flaring as grief?

I place it on the earth.

7.
Saying the Names

Today I visit the graves of my family,
so many lost to the world of light.
Yet so long as I come here they've not entirely vanished:
the bodies that the earth's reclaimed are dross;

spirits live beyond expired flesh.
I feel presence in their hovering absence;
a little faith in the imagination
and they shimmer with all the light beyond the grave.
I bow my head, walk from stone to stone,
murmuring each chiseled name.

Five: After the Summer

After the Summer

My neighbor's garden is dying: all the tended flowerbeds
strewn with debris, the sumptuous rose that flamed
through August withers on its scaffold of thorns.
By the fence sunflowers droop, their faces tattered,
their shadows thin like the shadows of the ravished,
the full-blown, in lonely hospices. Maples shed their leaves
in fevered heaps; summer trees—frail and gray—
mock us with winter gestures. Soon the pond will
freeze over and reflect the sun as a glimmering
point—the way the eyes of the dead are said
to retain a last dwindling speck of light...
I'm thinking how my neighbor Walter, who tested
positive last March, chose to plant and cultivate,
chose to nurture such vulnerable, transitory blooms.
I marvel at his steadfastness, his willingness to confront
recurrent wastage. Next spring when the world emerges
from the last snowfall and the warm light hovers
I'll see him—if he's here—working on his knees,
his head bowed, his hands moving in the deep earth.

Practicing the Dead Man's Float in Early Middle-Age

for my neighbor in remission

Because today will vanish
among the other days,
because it must soon
sink from sight
he savors the moments
drifting face-down
at the heart
of this blue pool,
as if suspended
between one life
and the next.
Dead Man's Float?
Sure, death lurks here—
drowned insects fleck
the water's surface,
the opossum that blundered
into headlights lies scrunched
in the road beyond
the fence, grass under-
foot parched by weeks
of implacable sun—nothing
changes that, but
for now the disease
(so opportunistic)
relents. For now he can roll
on his back, trees
shimmer their green
enticements, gulls
extend the moment
hovering midair. For

now a child paddles by,
laughing, bumping him
with her water-wings.
The both of them
doing what they need
to stay afloat.

Visiting Cousin Anna at the
Masonic Home for the Aged

There's a moment of panic
when I want to turn back
to the car and drive off.
But the old obligations
—or is it just guilt?—
keep me walking straight
down the path,
up the porch,
through chilled corridors
to where she waits among
the others who seem always
to be waiting, waiting...
The rec room's warm
and desperately cheerful
despite Ellie who's ranting
in her wheelchair, soaked
in fresh urine. Bruised
from a recent fall,
my spinster cousin's
a survivor, outliving
even the house where
she was born, demolished
now with blocks of others
to make space for the
township's new mall.
"They stole my home,"
she whispers because
the walls have ears,
the people on TV
can hear. One night
she'll dream of broken

escalators and tunnels
filled with endless stores
where shoppers, silent as
smiling mannequins, stand
frozen in fluorescent light.

Landscape with Querulous Couple

They were returning
from somewhere—
just the two of them
arguing in the car—
one wants to stop
at a motel for the night;
the other, who is driving,
wants to continue along
the mapped-out route
they've followed.
No stopovers.
No detours.
They are not lovers;
though one longs to be,
the other fears
a life beyond the
certainty of roadmaps.
Accusations. Denials.
Miles of deepening silence.
Till one lights a cigarette
& coughs. The other watches
the moon—red as a burning
tire—wobble over the highway.
The sky laden with stars,
faint & non-negotiable.

Senior Matinee

1.
Back Street
(Universal Pictures, 1961)

It always happens: the bungled phone call, gas gauge on empty,
missing by a hair's breadth that plane lifting off with your future.
Sometimes life makes these decisions for us, you muse and lose
yourself in your work, your art, placing happiness on hold. Years
pass. A chance encounter in a restaurant, on the street—you give
in to a swim at the beach, then that long shot of the ocean crash-
ing against the rocks... You take up residence on a block, fill
a house with stolen hours of pleasure, few and far between, but
someone gets hurt, someone innocent who never asked to be
part of the plot. In the end you retreat into the past, relive one
moment, over and over, when your world could have changed.
Though little, it is enough to sustain an almost perfect life,
ungrammatical, nearly real.

2.
Of Human Bondage
(RKO Pictures, 1934)

Philip never learns.
Time after time she betrays him
in the most callous, spiteful way.
Yet he keeps coming back for more.
Are you a damn glutton for punishment?
Open your eyes, love's never that blind!
you shout hopelessly at the b&w screen.
Doesn't he realize his physical impairment
is merely a manifestation of his crippled
spirit, that his club foot will be healed

once he grows strong enough to turn
and walk away from that bitch? But then
you remember your own version of this story:
You play Philip and Mildred's replaced
by Leigh whom you could never win, no matter
the gifts, the kindnesses lavished. Leigh always
distant and unmoved yet leaving the faintest
glimmer of hope that the life you envisioned
together was just a heart-of-stone's throw away.
Like Philip, you're willing to suffer a slew
of humiliations for the unlikely chance
that Leigh will grow to love you or at least sleep
with you. Like Mildred, Leigh's too self-absorbed
to give you a thought or a tumble. As in the film
this doomed relationship can only end in failure,
yet you keep Leigh's name in your cell phone,
knowing a sequence of numbers will allow you
to experience once again the agony and ecstasy
of human bondage.

3.
Angels Over Broadway
(Columbia Pictures, 1940)

We love the Damon Runyon characters:
the sleazy anti-hero, the vivacious Beauty,
the sad little thief intent on suicide,
even more it's the playwright, the fallen artist,
the drunken buffoon, who elicits our sympathies.
His art's in jeopardy, his marriage in the dumpster,
like the one behind that upscale nightclub where
the anti-hero counsels the unfazed Beauty

on his misbegotten plan to swindle the thief
out of an imaginary bundle at a crooked card game.
But the laughs on everyone until the tipsy playwright
somehow succeeds in ordering this madcap scenario
into a redemptive plot. We love the way the playwright
awakens out of his drunken stupor, returns to his life,
memory cleansed like a man given a clean slate to begin
again, oblivious to the masterwork he's created:
the thief safely rescued, the anti-hero redeemed
and reconciled with the Beauty at a greasy spoon
with its blue plate specials. When they whirl off
down the street, arm-in-arm, two angels over Broadway,
the audience claps and claps.

Dirty Frank's

I'd see her when she was hookin' out of Dirty Frank's
      west of the river
in that neighborhood of crowded tree streets—Locust,
      Spruce, Pine—
those blocks of bustling street life that loudly roll out
      to West Philly.
We'd wave, chat, down a few "Rusty Nails." *Stay safe, babe!*
      So young & pretty:
a black southern belle; her mother taught her hymns
      —I'll fly away—
she seemed out of place there like a saint in a shithole.
      I hadn't known
beauty could be so incongruous. Then she vanished.
      Around the time
the Rivera Exhibit opened at the Art Museum.
      I wondered
for a while where she'd gone, vaguely feared the worst:
      some random violence,
some tragic headline. Mostly though I was interested
      in surviving my own
life. Things had come to that… Months later I saw her
      on the street
under red blinking neon that stuttered Adam & Eve's
      Adult Pleasure Garden
near a vent where a man in his cardboard bed
      was slyly
jacking off in the steam. Her clothes disheveled;
      hair matted
thick as a nightmare. "Sheba-Rose!" She looked
      right through me.
I called again; she tried to focus like a drunken
      debutante negotiating

the Expressway's slick curves in fog. "It's me.
        From Dirty Frank's.
Remember?" She was so high on something
        I could've
been a trick, or a vent man, or a chauffeur from the Lord
        come to fetch
her home in that long limousine with the angelic sheen.
        Her belly
puffed like a miniature Buddha's on the shelf of some
        Chinese gift shop,
she moaned a garbled mantra I couldn't quite make out.
        I remember turning
away, then, the hiss of steam from that vent, a moon
        white as flowers
in Diego Rivera's "Nude with Calla Lilies." All around us
        cold wind
off the river and down on the corner some drag queens
        bitching
each other, eyeing the dark procession of cars.

In Early Evening

Any knock at the door
I slip into the shadows
inside the cedar closet—
pretend I'm not at home,

and should the phone ring I let
the answering machine pick up,
its long, digital memory
far better than my own.

Only when the house is empty,
perfectly still, will the voices
of my mother and sister return—
how beautiful their chatter,

though years ago I admonished
every distraction, every interruption,
shouting harshly from my desk
by the window, as the first star

of heaven kindled the night. Now
I'd beg to be privy to their lost
conversations. But they whisper:
Work, for the night is coming

So it's time to make my way
to the side yard, to the modest
vegetable garden where I failed
to entice whole heads of lettuce,

sweet ears of corn from the black
earth, where the orange flowered
zucchini did not thrive, but tomato
vines ran rampant all summer

and need cutting back.
I'll prune till the moon has risen.
I'll gather a few ripe tomatoes
in my hands, bless them

with sprays of water, stack them
in grandmother's carved fruit bowl,
the one made of frosted crystal.
Tomorrow the tall kitchen windows

will fill with clear morning light.

Filipina Rose,

only by chance
I learn of your death,
six years too late
to pick up a phone.
I google your name
—Rose Occena—
but *Oceana Rose*
keeps popping up.
It's a champagne-
colored flower,
spiral shaped,
slender stems.
I remember a
dusk that color
(so like your rouge):
we sat years ago
at an outdoor café
somewhere down
the Jersey shore.
You always wore
your heart on
your sleeve,
my dear,
& paid the price.
We toasted our
deadbeat dads
who dismissed us
from their lives,
never taught us
to speak *Visayon*—
our vibrant "Fuck you,
Dad!" forever

lost in translation.
Hours later we left
shit-faced & laughing…
I find your obit
online: *age 67,*
long hotel career,
survived by one
brother, two nieces,
& "Dildo" the dog.
Your story withers
to a few dark lines,
Rose Oceana.
Now I've confused
your name with that
shimmer of chiffon,
flamboyant flower
bred to produce a rose
with outstanding,
long-lasting blooms,
fabulous pastel
of an orange-
tinged white.

Pause En Route

You open your eyes:
it's the middle of your life.
Morning manifests itself
with flimsy light, a rain
grows monotonous.

Last day of your vacation.
You can't recall a memorable
moment of your stay
in this city you chose
by looking away and
jabbing a finger on a map.
"I just wanted to go someplace,"
you'll explain too often
to people who haven't asked.

In the Greyhound station
the paraplegic girl
in the wheelchair ignores
the man that keeps staring—
the one in the exterminator's suit,
SLUG-A-BUG printed on the back—
by perfecting pirouettes
in her imagination.

A bus pulls out and there's something
infinitely sad
in the shifting gears,
the deep thrum of motor.
You wonder whether you're arriving
or departing. For a moment
the voice of Rilke's ghost

blares out over the loudspeaker.

Sing jubilation and praise
  to assenting angels

Yeah, sure, you mutter,
dropping coins in the broken
vending machine, humming
lines to poems that haven't
been written, while someone,
disguised as himself, waves

to you from the crowd
dispersing in all directions
to pursue those solitary
engagements, the ones
we call our lives.

Poem Almost About Richard Hugo

Dear_____,

We spent a good hour or so talking
about poems & how Hugo presided
over that first book. I truly enjoyed
the chat, mentioned some reasons
I thought you were evolving into
your own poet, offered my congrats
on the teaching promotion, especially
on organizing the poetry festival.
Later that year I sent you a tape
of Hugo reading at SF State.
So the next summer when I waved
to you the first day of the Second
Annual Conference, why the snub?
I know how busy your itinerary
must be, how many students &
colleagues you must greet in a given
year, but it hurt to know that you
hadn't a clue as to who I might be, even
after you signed my copy of your book:
"To a kindred spirit whose company
and conversation I won't soon forget."
You stayed drunk & loud that whole
weekend; I heard you insult someone
as you staggered from a panel,
assisted by your wife. We never
spoke again. I remember Hugo
writing somewhere—maybe *31
Letters and 13 Dreams*—of going
off the deep end, driving drunk
through half a dozen states

to escape the trauma of success.
What price fame? Ask that poet
who kept his sanity by retreating
back to the "wind, sea and rain,"
the primal sources of his art. Then
ask me if I'll buy your next book.

No Map Can Hold the Wind

for Lisel Mueller

The ghostly girl kneels
at a window praying that
the Gestapo will release her
father who's been detained
a week. For seven days
she's learned to calm her nerves
by focusing on colors. She gazes
at the moon: sometimes
orange as a pumpkin;
tonight whiter than a skull.
This is Hamburg, 1939:
everywhere the spying children
of the Fuhrer, SS agents
tracking dissidents through
snow that fills
thin streets where
pine and spruce
toss in a frost
of moonlight...
From someone's radio
Hitler's voice explodes
as red as the swatch
of poppies the girl
saw bursting out in a field
one spring. His voice is bristling
like an angry flame; promises
drip like drops of blood
that blossom on the butcher's floor.
Der Anstreicher spricht
von kommenden grossen Zeiten
Trucks filled with soldiers

roar down the roads.
A cold wind's blowing
white mist so thick
the houses start to vanish.
No map can hold the wind
at bay; it blows away
all boundaries. It's late.
The girl drifts off
to bed and dreams
of a grinning skull,
the voice that hisses
like a flame, and snow
that won't stop falling—
turning, flake by smoldering
flake, into ashes from
the crematorium. Lord
of the Innocent, grant
that she awaken in the
morning, as if in a world
where war is forbidden,
the twisted arms of the
swastika straightened,
and her father returned
unharmed, save for the
bruises purpling his flesh
like a trail of footprints
darkening the snow.

"St Jerome Removing a Thorn from the Lion's Paw"

Zanetto Bugatto, 1461

I love this painting of you removing the thorn
From the lion's paw, oblivious to danger.
No wonder you are the patron saint
Of librarians, encyclopediasts, and other
Guardians of knowledge who must face
Whatever dangers stand before them in
Their efforts to serve the impervious
Public, a collective entity that can roar
Like the king of beasts or sit docile
As an oversized kitten ready to be
Nurtured by the service of another.

At the Library

"Irvington's a great place
not to live," says Richard
one of our regulars who's
spent his whole life
in this washed-up town.

He's gray, one eye filmed
over like a frozen pond.
All around him the streets
slowly succumbed to a blight
that left neighborhoods stunted:
factories shut down; stores
packed up, disappeared over-
night; theaters vanished
with their grand marquees…

Still the library survives
in these precincts of ruin,
this urban ghost town.

Day after day they come
perusing newspapers, surfing
the Net, checking-out books
from the dwindling collection.

Richard's obsessed
with historical victims—
the survivors of *Auschwitz,*
the *Gulag* Archipelago—
having survived a knife
to his throat when he
drove a night cab; he

requests bios of Beria,
Stalin's right-hand man,
who murdered whores
for fun, buried them
outside his home—"One
serial-killing-good-old
boy," he smiles with irony.

So different from that smile
in his high school yearbook
that I pull from a shelf out
of curiosity one day. He's
dark haired, clear-eyed,
handsome and grinning
in the company of the
other Irvington grads
staring straight at a future
now consigned to a chapter
in the history of this lonely
marginal town.

Grief

Years ago, naïve enough to tell
a friend whom I loved my feelings
I learned the attraction wasn't mutual,
and went the way of discarded things,
slowly becoming forgotten...

Not to say I haven't had mornings
written on a clean page of sky, oceans
of afternoons watching gulls float
like perfect punctuation in the wind,
evenings' coffers filling with coins
of moonlight...

Sadness pervades this life, but who
needs another sob story? People
go their way like strangers
in Chekhov's tale about the old
cabdriver whose son has died,
who has only his horse to turn
to. Remember how they huddled,
snow falling flake by flake by flake . . .

Alexei

after Cavafy

Perhaps to check a date,
maybe out of boredom,
I skimmed through a history
of the House of Romanov

last night. Though late
one page led to the next,
decades passed in so few
paragraphs. That lost

world of palace and pomp,
those figures at the heart
of such tragic grandeur
posing for a family shot:

the Tsar and Tsaritsa,
their daughters, the grand
duchesses, in immaculate
white dresses, stare regally,

eerily into the photographer's
camera to preserve this moment
of perfect Russian autocracy.
I would have closed the book

had it not been for the small
boy in sailor suit wedged
between two sisters. O,
Alexei, son of Nicholas,

prince and heir to the throne
history will never allow you,
disaster lurks like Rasputin
in shadows beyond the photo's

edges. I turned more pages
to find you a few years older
in military garb, handsome
as a toy soldier and as fragile—

so easily bruised, one nick
could start a geyser of blood
that would not halt until the
strange monk prayed above you.

What is more dangerous
the surge of blood that won't
clot within the veins or the surge
of rebellion that won't be

quelled on the streets outside?
I wanted you to survive the snows
of Siberia, to escape the *Bolsheviks*
on the Polar Star, sailing far

from the nest of assassins,
their edict of blood! blood! blood!
So I imagined you grown
beyond that Revolution—

athletic and distinguished,
the love of many lives.
When I fell asleep I dreamed
you entered the room,

your face worn and ghostly,
stricken with the knowledge
of a dying dynasty, wearing
the same look as in that cellar

the last moments of your life,
still hoping they might show
mercy, the swine who wrote
in blood upon the wall:

This night Balthazar was
murdered by his slaves

"Autumn: Hounds, Game, Fruit and Vegetables"

—Alexandre Francois Desportes, c.1712

1.
Like so much I stumble onto in this life—for instance, the girl
in the green satin gown weeping by the fountain of waterlilies
in the rain, or that poem by the Chinese poetess
lost in some forgotten anthology that makes me
whisper: *O, Princess Le-Chang, human life is hard—*
I found by chance the Desportes painting hanging in
Musee Des Beaux-Arts De Montreal. The ghost
of old hunts fills that space the artist chose to paint.

2.
Two hounds—one slyly crouching to lap the hare's
warm blood, the other snarling to guard his master's
spoils—contend on either side of the rich brown pelt
flung upon the piled squash and celery, greens
gathered from the fields, potpourri of clustered grapes,
plums that shimmer in tight skins, the rosy cheeks
of peaches polished in the sun. But terror burns
in the dead hare's eye, staring out of history:
death at the heart of harvest, blood before the feast.
A careful hand has hung the pheasants upside down,
nailed them like decrees to the thick bark of a tree.
One feather falls through centuries...

3.
I was so alone that fall I drove my mother to Montreal.
She mostly slept on prescription drugs that week
in a city she'd later recall only by moonlight. I had
mornings, afternoons to myself: I roamed bilingual
streets, outdoor cafes—applauding *chansonniers*—
lingered in the corridors of art galleries and museums.

We had so little time. I had to learn the brute fact
that for every plenitude, every bounty, there is a price
the world exacts. Amid the grace of this northern city
my mother's paranoia flared, calmed only by her meds.

4.
In the painting the fruit and vegetable arrangements
suggest a world of order, restraint. A place my mother
could feel safe in. The hounds are there to protect her,
though the blood of the innocent may excite them,
but can that shining harvest stave off the fear and anger
she suffers, silence the conspiratorial voices of the hunt?
I know what lurks beneath such amplitudes; I know
my mother will grow distrustful of this cornucopia.
The hare's eye is the dead center of the painting;
everything arranges itself around that one unalterable fact.

My Cat and I Sit Out on the Balcony after Dinner, Watching the Sunset and Pretending We're Famous Poets

I feel like Cavafy done with another day's
tedium, proofreading letters in English
at his Irrigation Office, Alexandria, 1911—

except I've spent my day in New Jersey
a century later, engaged in the equally
tedious task of editing MARC records.

Moon reminds me of Li Po as she sits
quietly staring at nothing while the crickets
gather, rehearsing their evening song.

"She's dwelling in the moment," as my Buddhist
buddy would say, and I envy the ease with which
she's free of the ten thousand stressful things.

"Little Li Po," I whisper. She turns
her head, stifles a yawn, gives me a look
of infinite bemusement, as if to say: *Li Po?*

Right. Now get real—hello???
We return to our own meditations;
the sun floats above us like a red pavilion

on a mountain somewhere in *Szechwan,* 760 A.D.,
old monks, sure-footed as cats, climbing paths
toward the painted clouds and waterfalls.

Identity

"We are Thai, Filipino, Vietnamese.
We are, all of us, post exotics"
　　　　　　　　—Eugene Gloria

Growing up *mestizo*—
half-Filipino, half-white—
I hated people always asking
my nationality before my name.
How was a five year old
supposed to answer? Why?
By the time I was twelve
I let them think whatever:
"Yes, I'm Chinese, Japanese,
Hawaiian, Indian, Thai,
Vietnamese, Cambodian."
"Yes, I'm a Korean war baby."
"Yes, I'm an Eskimo (sans igloo)."
In childhood my mixed-race
was a stigma that shamed me.
In adulthood it became some-
thing exotic. People told me
how lucky I was to be
the progeny of two worlds.
I faked a dumb-ass
smile and said nothing.
All those documents—
surveys, applications—
of Officialdom that demand
ethnic information, left
me ambivalent: do I check
off "Asian" or "White"?
Now Eugene, that hip *flip*,
connoisseur of Chinese takeout,
defines us with a new term.

Thanks, *Kaibigan*; yeah,
it works for me, Cous.
I can't wait for the next
census survey when I
bypass all the old
categories of ethnicity,
place my "X" next to
"Other" and write in glorious
yellow magic marker:
"American Post Exotic."

Hong Kong, Mississippi

"You don't sound like where you from,
I know—you from Hong Kong, Mississippi!"
—Bo Diddley

You won't get there by map,
no matter how long you pore
over one. Consult any road
atlas, as if an astrological
chart, you'll still draw up a blank.
There are no demographics
offered by the U.S. Census, no
State guide books to reference
your journey into the delta.
Word of mouth would be best,
but who can trust language?
Besides, local residents all keep
a tight lip; they sound
and look like typical inhabitants.
Who would guess they're not?
Only the truly conflicted,
for whom incongruity wounds,
will sense the powers they wield,
the mysticism that shrouds
their down-home Shangri-La.
Only pure desperation leads
to this place of healing,
where the image in your mind
matches the face in your mirror,
and the shame-dragon's driven
at long last away. The desperate
will know what turn to make
at the crossroads to nowhere,
the one back road to follow
out to the bridge that collapsed

years ago in a loud cloud of dust,
yet still can be crossed if paid
its full toll of grief. Few will
arrive at that town lost
in the fields of cotton,
its temples and pagodas
shimmering in the sun
like a *Taoist* painting where
Buddha transcends the blues,
watching a white butterfly rise
and enter the moment.

Notes

Adobo: In Filipino cuisine a variety of marinated beef, pork or chicken.

Alaskeros: Filipino immigrants who worked the salmon canneries of Alaska as seasonal laborers during the 1930s and 1940s.

Carabao: Tagalog word for water buffalo.

"Der Anstreicher spricht von kommenden grossen Zeiten: The house-painter speaks of great times to come." (trans. from the German)

"Flip": Racist term for a Filipino in the United States.

Illocano: Refers both to an indigenous dialect of the Philippine Islands and to one who speaks that dialect.

Kaibigan: Tagalog word for friend.

Krasang: Tree which has long thorns on its bark and bears a sour nut-like fruit which Cambodian villagers frequently add to soups.

Lumpia: In Filipino cuisine an appetizer similar to a spring roll.

Pinoys: Filipino immigrants who entered America as laborers during the early 1930s.

Schenley: Inexpensive brand of American whiskey.

Sotanghon: In Filipino cuisine a type of long, transparent rice noodle.

Tagalog: Primary indigenous dialect of the Philippine Islands.

Utapats: Cambodian term meaning evildoers.

Visayan: An indigenous dialect spoken by Filipinos on the island of Cebu.

About the Author

Alfred Encarnacion has taught writing at Temple University and published poetry, short stories, essays, and literary reviews in journals such as *Crab Orchard Review, Florida Review, Indiana Review, North American Review, Paterson Literary Review, and The Virtual Artists Collective* (online review). He has won a Wilson Foundation Scholarship Award, a Poets House Scholarship in NYC, and his work has been nominated for a Pushcart Prize. His debut book of poetry, *The Outskirts of Karma,* appeared in 2012. He is currently the director of the Stratford Public Library in New Jersey.

Made in the USA
Middletown, DE
26 September 2016